I·N·S·I·D·E

INDIA

Prodeepta Das

Franklin Watts

London · New York · Sydney · Toronto

CONTENTS

© 1990 Franklin Watts
96 Leonard Street
London EC2 4HA

Franklin Watts Inc.
387 Park Avenue South
New York, N.Y. 10016

Franklin Watts Australia
14 Mars Road
Lane Cove
NSW 2066

Design: K & Co
Illustrations: Hayward Art Group

UK ISBN: 0 7496 0114 0
US ISBN: 0-531-14045-8
Library of Congress Catalog
Card Number: 89-49477

Phototypeset by Lineage Ltd,
Watford

Printed in Belgium

Front cover: Prodeepta Das
Back cover: Roy Curtis of the Chris
Fairclough Colour Library
Frontispiece: Prodeepta Das

Additional photographs: All taken
by Prodeepta Das except for the
following: Camera Press 8T;
Hutchison Library: 28, Alan
Hutchison 6, Michael Macintyre 7,
Chris Oldroyd 19; Popperfoto 8B;
Bartholomew/Frank Spoore
Pictures 9.

The land

The Union of India is the world's seventh largest country, but only China has a larger population. India is about 3,200 km (2,000 miles) from north to south, and 2,740 km (1,700 miles) from east to west. It has coasts along the Arabian Sea and the Bay of Bengal. The world's highest mountains, the Himalayas, lie to the north and northeast.

The broad northern plains of India are drained by the Ganges and Brahmaputra rivers. The northern plains have rich soils. They are India's most densely populated region. Much of southern India is a plateau called the Deccan. Bordering the plateau are two ranges called the Western and Eastern Ghats.

Below: **From Kashmir in the north, there are breathtaking views of the Himalayas, the world's tallest mountain range.**

Right: **Calcutta lies on the River Hooghly, a branch of the Ganges. It has made Calcutta important for trade.**

Below: **Rivers in the south like this one in the state of Tamil Nadu can dry up if rains fail.**

The Himalayas protect India from the freezing winds that sweep across Asia from the north in winter. They also stand in the path of the moisture laden monsoon winds that blow from the Arabian Sea and the Bay of Bengal. These winds usually bring heavy rain to India between June and September. October to February is the cool season, and March to the end of June is the hot season.

India has a tropical monsoon climate, although local differences exist. India's only desert is the Thar Desert in the northwest. It receives less than 25 cm (9.8 inches) of rain a year, while the Assam hills in the northeast receive more than 1,100 cm (433 inches) of rain a year.

Above: **The Thar Desert in the northwestern state of Rajasthan is a dry region. Camels are used for transport.**

The people and their history

The name India comes from the Indus River, where a major civilization flourished in about 2500 BC. People called Aryans ended this civilization in about 1500 BC. They started the caste system, which still survives today. Under this system, people were born into castes, or social groups, which were identified with certain occupations.

In the 3rd century BC, Chandragupta Maurya became the first king to unite India. His grandson Asoka extended the empire from southern India to Afghanistan. India came under Islamic rule when Muslims invaded India in the 12th century AD. The Muslim Mogul empire was founded in 1526. Its emperor, Akbar, brought peace between Muslims and Hindus in the 16th century.

Below: **Ancient monuments like the Buddhist Ajanta cave temples contain paintings that show how people used to live.**

Above: **On 15 August 1947 India became independent and Earl Mountbatten, Viceroy of India, declared Jawaharalal Nehru as the first Prime Minister.**

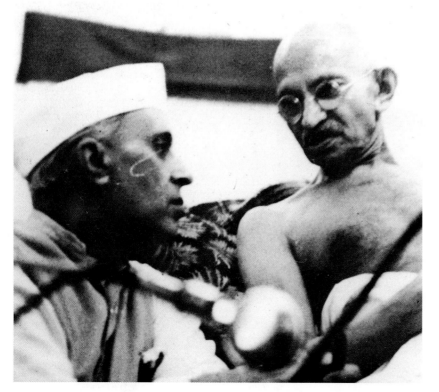

Left: **Mahatma Gandhi and Nehru were the two most prominent freedom fighters.**

From the 17th century, the British East India Company gradually took over India. In 1857, the Indian people rebelled. The British defeated the rebels, and in 1858 the British government made India part of their empire.

After World War I, a former lawyer, Mahatma Gandhi, led a non-violent struggle for Indian independence. India won its freedom on August 15, 1947 and Jawaharalal Nehru became the first prime minister of the new federal republic. The British India split into two nations, the mainly Hindu India and the mainly Muslim Pakistan. India has 14 major languages and more than 1,000 minor ones. This is a major cause of some of India's political problems.

Below: **V.P. Singh, leader of the National Front Party, was elected Prime Minister of India in November 1989.**

Towns and cities

About three out of every four people in India live in small farming villages. Many farming families are poor, although living conditions in many villages have improved, through the supply of electricity, communications, transport, and better health and educational services. However, many people have left the villages in the hope of finding a better life in the cities. As a result, many cities have become overcrowded and unemployment has become a serious problem.

India now has 2 cities with more than a million people. The three largest cities are, in order of size, Calcutta, Bombay, and Greater Delhi, which includes India's capital New Delhi.

Below: **Villages in India have a strong community feeling.**

Above: **Puri, a town on the East coast, is a seaside resort as well as a place of pilgrimage. It attracts many visitors.**

Left: **In Bombay, where living space is limited, the luxury apartments of the rich can be found alongside the slums of the very poorest people.**

11

Greater Delhi includes two distinct areas: Old and New Delhi. Old Delhi's ancient buildings include the Qutab Minar, a 71m (234ft) high stone tower. The Lal Qila, or Red Fort, consists of palaces surrounded by huge red sandstone walls. It was built in 1648. Old Dehli also contains the Jama Masjid, India's largest mosque.

Sir Edwin Lutyens, a British architect, designed many of the buildings in New Delhi. They included the Central Secretariat and the Rashtrapati Bhavan, formerly the British Viceroy's palace and now the home of India's president. Another reminder of British influence is Connaught Place, the main shopping area.

Below: **The Secretariat designed by the British architect Lutyens is one of many impressive buildings in New Delhi.**

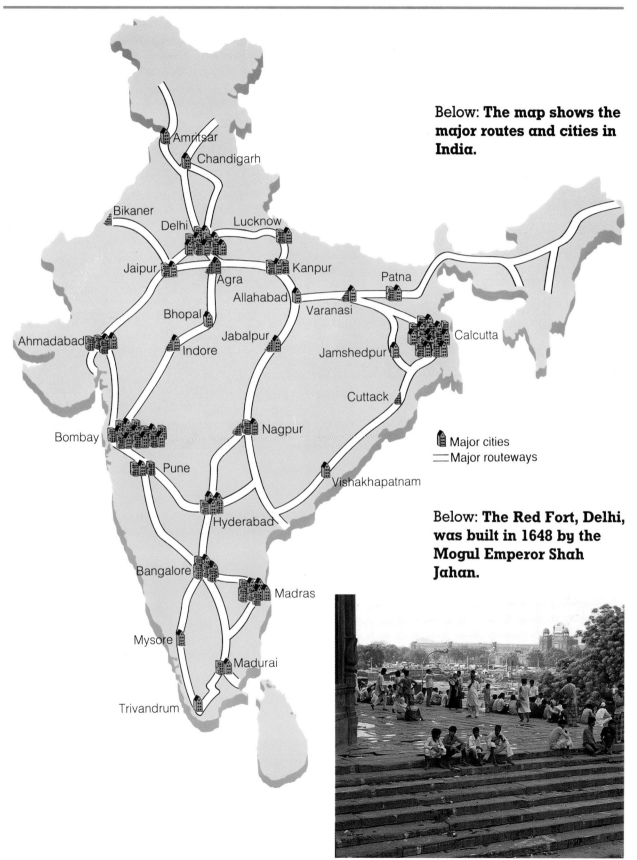

Below: **The map shows the major routes and cities in India.**

Amritsar
Chandigarh
Bikaner
Delhi
Lucknow
Jaipur
Agra
Kanpur
Patna
Allahabad
Bhopal
Varanasi
Jabalpur
Calcutta
Indore
Jamshedpur
Ahmadabad
Cuttack
Nagpur
Bombay
Vishakhapatnam
Pune
Hyderabad
Bangalore
Madras
Mysore
Madurai
Trivandrum

🏛 Major cities
— Major routeways

Below: **The Red Fort, Delhi, was built in 1648 by the Mogul Emperor Shah Jahan.**

Calcutta is a river port, about 145 km (90 miles) from the Bay of Bengal. It was founded in the 1690s. It grew rapidly when refugees arrived during the division of India in 1947, and the war that led to East Pakistan becoming Bangladesh in 1971. Many people are homeless. Mother Teresa won the Nobel Peace prize for her work with the poor of Calcutta.

Bombay is a port on the Arabian Sea. It is the commercial capital of India and one of Asia's busiest ports. Cotton and other textile industries developed in Bombay under British rule. Today, Bombay claims 40 percent of India's textile industries and 15 percent of the country's factories. Bombay is also India's film capital.

Below: **Victoria Memorial in Calcutta, now a museum, houses many important relics of the British Empire. Calcutta was the capital of British India between 1773 and 1911.**

Family life

Above: **Mealtimes, as in this tribal household, are a time for all family members to be together.**

In the villages, the people continue the old tradition of parents and their children sharing the same house as grandparents and, sometimes, other relatives. By contrast, large family groups seldom live together in cities. This is because accommodation is scarce and expensive. But most people treasure family life. During festivals, many townspeople return to their family village for a reunion.

Old people are especially important in Indian families. Parents teach their children to respect old people for their wisdom and experience. Many Indian children have to work to earn money for the home, but primary education is compulsory.

Left: **In such cities as Bombay, well-off families live in small apartments like those in the West.**

Below: **Many families do not have their own water supply and have to depend on public taps in the street.**

Food

Food varies a great deal from region to region. Most people in the south are vegetarian, coastal people eat fish, and those who live inland eat more meat. Muslims do not eat pork, and Hindus do not eat beef. Goat meat is popular. In northern India, many people eat chapati or naan, two kinds of bread made from wheat flour, with their meals, but in the south most people eat rice instead.

Indian "curry" includes any fish, meat, and vegetable dish prepared with a spicy gravy. Popular spices include cardamom, cinnamon, cloves, coriander, garlic, ginger and turmeric. "Tandoori" dishes consist of food cooked in a special clay oven called a tandoor.

Below: **People bring things from far and wide to sell in the market.**

Above: **Tandoori chicken, naan and salad are a popular dish.**

Left: **Indian markets sell a large variety of vegetables, tropical fruits and household items.**

Sports and pastimes

India is a major sporting nation. It has won international recognition in badminton, cricket, field hockey, soccer, squash and tennis. Its athletes have won many medals in Olympic, Asian and Commonwealth games. Yoga is a form of traditional Indian exercise. It has become a popular form of relaxation and keeping fit throughout the world.

India has many festivals all year round. Diwali, a Hindu festival to celebrate the goddess of wealth and beauty, and Holi, a spring festival, are enjoyed by adults and children. India is the world's largest film-producing nation. Going to the movies is a major Indian pastime. Movies with songs and dances are particularly popular.

Below: **Cricket is a popular game. Children in remote villages can be seen playing it their way.**

Left: **The festival of Dussera, held in October each year, is one of many popular Hindu festivals.**

Below: **Cinema hoardings are everywhere. Hundreds of films in Hindi and regional languages are produced every year.**

The arts

Three world religions – Buddhism, Islam and Hinduism – have greatly influenced the arts of India. The *vedas*, or sacred hymns, are the oldest Indian literature. They were composed around 1500 BC. Two epics, the *Ramayana* and *Mahabharata* were written around 1000 BC. The *Mahabharata* tells of a war between five princes and their hundred cousins. These epics and the *vedas* were written in Sanskrit, which forms the basis of many north Indian languages. Tamil is the basis of south Indian languages.

Modern Indian writers include the novelist Prem Chand (1880-1936) and the Nobel prize winner for literature, Sir Rabindranath Tagore (1861-1941). Some of Tagore's stories have been filmed by director Satyajit Ray.

Below: **This painting of Hanuman, the monkey god, is an example of early Indian Hindu art. Many old paintings and carvings are religious.**

Examples of the influence of religion on art and architecture can be found all over India in temples, palaces and mosques. The Ajanta Caves contain beautiful, early, Buddhist wall paintings dating from between 100 BC and AD 600. Rajasthani miniature paintings from the 16th century depict scenes from the Hindu epics in vivid detail. The Taj Mahal was built as a mausoleum by the Mogul ruler Shah Jahan (1592-1666) for his wife Mumtaz Mahal.

Indian classical dance tells a story with movements of hands and feet and gestures of the eyes and eyebrows. *Natya Sastra*, India's first book on dance and drama, was written between 300 BC and AD 200.

Above: **This dancer is performing *Odissi*, a classical Indian dance which is over 700 years old.**

Farming

Farming employs more than 60 percent of the people. Since 1947, farm production has increased dramatically, largely as a result of a special policy called the Green Revolution. This has involved improved irrigation and flood control, the use of special fast-growing varieties of crops, and the greater use of fertilizers and pesticides. The government encourages farmers to invest in tractors and other machinery, but many are too poor to do this.

The major crops are rice in the south and wheat in the north. Other crops include coffee, cotton, oilseeds, beans and tea. Cows are kept as work animals, but Hindus do not eat beef. Cows are a major source of milk. Sea fishing is also important.

Below: **Rice is the staple food of many Indians. It grows in wet regions.**

Above: **In many parts of India, bullocks are still used to till the land.**

Left: **Picking tea leaves needs special care. India's Darjeeling and Assam teas are drunk worldwide.**

Industry

India has many natural resources. It produces about 60 percent of the oil that it needs. The main oilfields are in Assam and off the coast near Bombay. India also has large reserves of coal, iron ore, bauxite, copper and other minerals.

Since India became independent, it has developed many industries. Great dams have been built to produce hydroelectric power, while nuclear power stations and stations using fuels have been built to produce electricity. Since 1947, the electricity supply has increased by 15 times. Some of the Indian companies involved in the oil and gas and electrical industries are among the biggest in the world.

Below: **Both offshore and inshore oil explorations are carried out to meet the country's oil needs.**

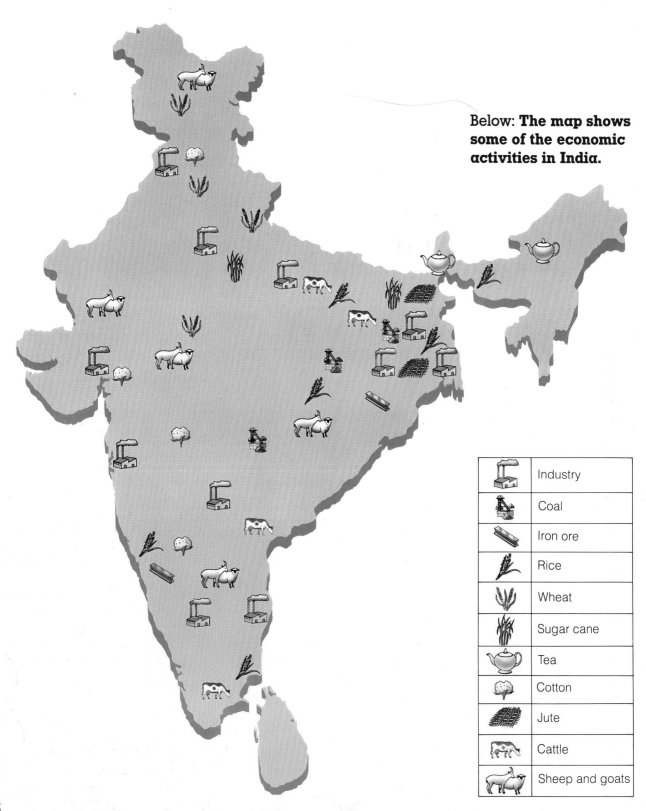

Below: The map shows some of the economic activities in India.

	Industry
	Coal
	Iron ore
	Rice
	Wheat
	Sugar cane
	Tea
	Cotton
	Jute
	Cattle
	Sheep and goats

India leads the world in producing cotton yarn. More than 9 million people work in this industry. The rail system is another major employer. India also has huge iron and steel mills, and the steel is used to make many products, including bicycles, cars, machinery, sewing machines and tractors. The handicraft industry is also important. Many craft industries are small and based in the home.

Much of India's recent success in building up industries owes much to the work of scientists and researchers. Scientific research has enabled India to develop space technology, computers, microchips and telecommunications industries, including the production of radios and television sets.

Below: **Cotton yarn and fabric is one of India's leading exports. It is produced all over India both in fully modernized factories and in village huts on small hand looms.**

Looking to the future

India faces many problems. For example, its population is growing quickly, partly because of improved health services. Population growth has led to overcrowding, poverty and unemployment.

India is also a country whose people are divided by language and religion. Some groups would like to break away from India and create their own countries. For example, violence has occurred in the northwestern Punjab region, where some followers of the Sikh religion have wanted to set up their own state, called Khalistan. India has border problems with China and Pakistan and clashes have occurred in frontier regions.

Above: **The Golden Temple of Amritsar, the Sikh religion's holiest shrine, was stormed by the army in 1984 and led to Prime Minister Indira Gandhi's assassination by Sikh terrorists.**

India is one of the world's 25 poorest countries. But it has made great economic progress since it won its independence in 1947. For example, food production has increased, on average, at a faster rate than the population. As a result, Indians are now better fed, and when droughts ruin crops, the country has large supplies of food available for starving people.

Despite all its problems, India has remained a democracy, with an elected national parliament consisting of two houses, and elected assemblies in each of its 25 states. Everyone aged 18 or over can vote and India can boast that it is the world's largest democratic country. Indians enjoy arguing about politics and criticizing their leaders. But they understand that their governments are trying to do in a few years what took many other countries far longer to achieve.

Below: **Government-sponsored advertisements promote the use of birth control methods as a way to reduce India's rapid rate of population growth.**

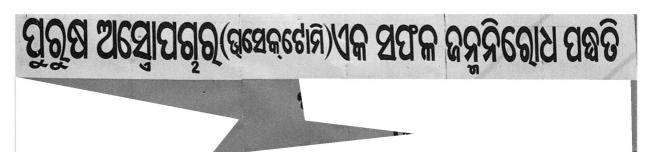

ପୁରୁଷ ଅସ୍ତ୍ରୋପଚାର୍‌(ଭ୍ୟାସେକ୍‌ଟୋମି)ଏକ ସଫଳ ଜନ୍ମନିରୋଧ ପଦ୍ଧତି

Facts about India

Area:
3,287,590 sq km
(1,269,218 sq miles)

Population:
817.4 million (1989
estimated)

Capital:
New Delhi

Largest cities:
(population includes
cities and suburbs)
Delhi 5,714,000
Bombay 8,227,000
Calcutta 9,166,000
Madras 4,277,000

Official languages:
Hindi
15 Official State
languages

Religions:
Hinduism: 83 percent;
Islam 11 percent;
Christianity 2.6
percent; Sikhism 1.9
percent; Buddhism 0.9
percent.

Main exports:
Textiles, leather
products, chemicals,
tea

Unit of currrency:
Rupee

India compared with other countries

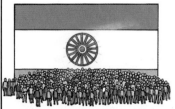

India 244 per sq km

Britain 232 per sq km

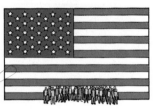

USA 26 per sq km

Australia 2 per sq km

Above: **How many people?**
India is one of the world's
most densely populated
countries.

Below: **How large? India is**
the world's seventh
largest country.

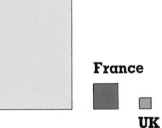

France

USA   **India**   **UK**

Below: **Indian money and stamps.**

AFGHANISTAN

CHINA

Jammu and Kashmir
Cease fire line

Srinagar

Amritsar
Jullundur
Ludhiana
Chandigarh
Dehra Dun

Saharanpur

Meerut
Delhi
New Dehli
Moradabad
Himalayas
NEPAL
BHUTAN

Bikaner
Barelly
Aligarh

PAKISTAN

Thar desert
Jaipur
Agra
R. Jumna
Lucknow
Gorakhpur
R. Brahmaputra

Ajmer
Jodhpur
Gwalior
Kanpur
Patna
R. Ganges

Kota
Jhansi
Allahabad
Varanasi
BANGLADESH

Dhanbad
Asansol

Ahmadabad
Ujjain
Bhopal
Jabalpur
Ranchi
Durgapur

Jamnagar
Vadodara
Indore
Jamshedpur
Haora
Calcutta
BURMA

Rajkot
R. Narmada
Raurkela

Bhavnagar
Surat
Amraoti
Raipur

Nasik
Nagpur
Durg
Cuttack
R. Mahanadi

Aurangabad

Thana
Ulhasnagar
R. Godavari
Bay of Bengal

Bombay
Pune

Warangal
Visakhapatnam
Andaman Island
(India)

Sholapur
Deccan
Hyderabad

Kolhapur
Sangli
R. Krishna
Rajahmundry

Vijayawada
Guntur

Arabian Sea

Belgaum

Hubli
Eastern Ghats

Mangalore
Bangalore
Madras

Mysore

Salem
Pondicherry

Calicut
R. Cauvery

Coimbatore
Tiruchirapalli
Nicobar Islands
(India)

Cochin
Madurai

Maldive Islands
(India)

Tirunelveli
Trivandrum
Tuticorin

Western Ghats

MALDIVE ISLANDS

**SRI
LANKA**

Indian Ocean

Index